31 verses

CHRIST

every

teenager

should

know

NEW HOPE®
P U B L I S H E R S
Imprint of Iron Stream Media

Birmingham, Alabama

Other books in the
31 Verses Every Teenager Should Know series

Identity　　　　　　*The Way*
Love　　　　　　　*Sequence*
Rooted　　　　　　*Christ*

New Hope® Publishers
100 Missionary Ridge
Birmingham, AL 35242
NewHopePublishers.com
An imprint of Iron Stream Media
IronStreamMedia.com

New Hope Publishers serves its authors as they express their views, which may not express the views of the publisher.

Library of Congress Cataloging-in-Publication Data has been filed

All scripture quotations, unless otherwise indicated, are taken from the Holy Bible, New International Version®, NIV®. Copyright © 1973, 1978, 1984, 2011 by Biblica, Inc.™ Used by permission of Zondervan. All rights reserved worldwide. www.zondervan.com The "NIV" and "New International Version" are trademarks registered in the United States Patent and Trademark Office by Biblica, Inc.™

ISBN-13: 978-1-56309-418-7
Ebook ISBN: 978-1-56309-419-4
　　　　　　　1 2 3 4 5—24 23 22 21 20

Contents

Introduction

Who would you say is the most important person you know? You probably know about a lot of celebrities or sports figures, but the odds are that you *really* don't know them. You've heard about them and even read about them, but do you know them? You may know all the words to their songs, all their sports stats, and whom they're dating. But do you know them? Maybe you've even met them, but I'll bet that it was only a brief introduction. You probably don't have a relationship with them. You don't *really* know them.

But what about Jesus? Jesus is the most important person of all time. Even before He was born, people were looking for Him. And the world has never been the same since He arrived. Even our historic calendar is centered on Him; B.C. means "before Christ." Now, you might know *about* Jesus, but do you really know Him? After reading this book, you will definitely know more about Jesus, but that is not the only purpose of this book. This book is designed to invite you into a relationship with Him.

If you read all the devotions in this book, you will see that even before Jesus was born, people were expecting Him. The prophets of the Old Testament wrote about Jesus hundreds of years before His birth. Some 2,000 years later, people are still talking about Jesus.

Jesus wants to have a relationship with you. If you read this book knowing that the most important person ever desires to have a relationship with you, your time will be well spent.

How to Use This Book

Now that you own this incredible little book, you may be wondering, "What do I do with it?"

Glad you asked. The great thing about this book is you can use it just about any way you want. It's not a system. It's a resource that can be used in ways that are as unique and varied as you are. A few suggestions …

The One-Month Plan
On this plan, you'll read one devotional each day for a month. This is a great way to immerse yourself in the Bible for a monthlong period. (Okay, we realize every month doesn't have thirty-one days. But twenty-eight or thirty is close enough to thirty-one, right?) The idea is to cover a lot of information in a short amount of time.

The Scripture Memory Plan
The idea behind this plan is to memorize the verse for each day's devotion; you don't move on to the next devotion until you've memorized the Scripture you're on. If you're like most people, this might take you more than one day per devotion. So this plan takes a slower approach.

The "I'm No William Shakespeare" Plan
Don't like to write or journal? This plan is for you. Listen, not everyone expresses themselves the same way. If you don't like to express yourself through writing, that's okay. Simply read

the devotion for each verse, then read the questions. Think about them. Pray through them. But don't feel as if you have to journal if you don't want to.

The Strength in Numbers Plan

God designed humans for interaction. We're social creatures. How cool would it be if you could go through *Christ* with your friends? Get a group of friends together. Consider agreeing to read five verses each week, then meeting to talk about them.

Pretty simple, right? Choose a plan. Or make up your own. But get started already. What are you waiting for?

Verse 1

For God so loved the world that he gave his one and only Son, that whoever believes in him shall not perish but have eternal life.

—John 3:16

In the last few years there have been some high-profile stories of mining accidents in the news. Many of these involved mineshafts collapsing, trapping miners thousands of feet below the earth's surface. Can you imagine how helpless those miners must have felt? There was nothing they could do to save themselves. They knew that help could only come from someone else.

Have you ever felt completely helpless? I don't mean the way you felt when you didn't study for a test or when you walked out of the restroom with toilet paper stuck to your shoe. I'm talking about claustrophobic-like helplessness. (No, that is not the fear of Santa Claus.) If you have ever felt this way, you know it's no fun.

Read John 3:9–16. Nicodemus was a really smart guy. He knew the laws and history of Israel. So Jesus reminded him of a story found in Numbers 21 about a group of helpless Israelites wandering in the desert. Soon they got restless and started cursing Moses and God (which is never a good idea). Before they knew it, poisonous snakes had swarmed their camp, and lots of people were dying from being bitten. The Israelites begged God to save them. In response, God told Moses to raise a bronze snake on a stick so that when people were bitten, they could look at it and be healed.

Jesus retold this story to make a point. He wanted to relate to Nicodemus how He Himself had to be raised up—not on a stick, but on a cross in order to save the world. Jesus' purpose was to rescue the world from sin.

Like miners stuck in a mineshaft, we are all trapped and helpless in our sin. We need a savior. We can't make it out without one. Incredibly, God loved us so much that He gave us *the* Savior in the form of His only Son, Jesus. The Son of God came here for one reason: to save the world because the world could not save itself.

Why do you think God saved the Israelites? Why do you think God sent Jesus to save us?

_____

_____

What's the difference between helping people because they asked and helping people because you love them?

_____

_____

Think about a time from this past year when you couldn't do something by yourself. You needed someone to do it for you. Who was it that helped you, and why did he or she do that?

_____

_____

Verse 2

Today in the town of David a Savior has been born
to you; he is the Messiah, the Lord.

—Luke 2:11

If you've ever been on an overnight camping trip, then
you've probably sat outside and gazed up at a sky full of bril-
liant stars. Some nights, if you are away from the city, you can
see a countless number of stars. Most of the time, you probably aren't expecting to see anything out of the ordinary up
there. But if you've ever seen a shooting star or comet, then
you know what an awesome surprise that is! And surprises
like that are much better than you could have imagined.

Read Luke 2:1–12. Can you imagine how the shepherds felt
that night? There they were, counting sheep and stars, mind-
ing their own business—when suddenly the skies opened up
and an angel appeared. You know they were terrified because
the angel introduced himself by saying, "Do not be afraid. I
bring you good news." If I were a shepherd that night, I would
have needed some good news to keep from fainting. The angel
then told them that a Savior had been born and that He was
the Messiah. This was not just good news—it was great news!

For hundreds of years, the Israelites had been looking
for the Messiah to come and save them. Now here he was!

After generations and generations of waiting, the Messiah had finally come. But they didn't expect to find their promised King sleeping in a manger. Rather, the Israelites expected the Messiah to establish His rule immediately and with a mighty hand that would make them into a great nation. But God had different plans—better plans. His plan was that Jesus would rule through sacrifice, humility, and selflessness. Therefore, He came to this world as the image of love. Think about it: There is nothing more loving than a newborn child. So that is how Jesus arrived and that is how He established His rule.

The way that the Israelites least expected Jesus to appear was far better than they could have imagined.

How does your family usually spend Christmas? Do you eat specific things for Christmas dinner? Do you travel?

_____

_____

Now think of a Christmas from the past few years in which something unexpected happened. Did it make Christmas better for you and your family? How so?

_____

_____

You probably expect God to speak to you in a few ways that you're used to. Ask God to do something unexpected today that shows you in a fresh way how much He loves you.

_____

_____

_____

Verse 3

"The days are coming," declares the LORD, "when I will raise up for David a righteous Branch, a King who will reign wisely and do what is just and right in the land."

—Jeremiah 23:5

Other than the lack of modern medicine and the frequent use of beheading, it would be cool to travel back in time to see how great kings and queens ruled. But whether you're watching *King Arthur* or *The Lord of the Rings*, at least one truth cuts across all the portrayals of kingship: all the kings died. No matter how powerful a king might be or how far his kingdom expands, he still dies at some point in his rule. Although the people chant, "Long live the king!" the reality is that his term is only temporary.

Read Jeremiah 23:5–6. The prophet Jeremiah told the people of Israel that a king would come from the line of King David. This king would reign with wisdom and do what is right in the land. The people longed for this good king. Earthly kings came and went for Israel, and so far no one had been the great king they were looking for.

Then Jesus was born from the lineage of David. At last their good king had come! But Israel was under Roman rule at this time. That meant one thing: Jesus was not to be an earthly and political king—but rather an eternal and universal king. Jesus' rule was not just over the Israelites—but over all people. Jesus fulfilled Jeremiah's prophecy of a coming king who would be wise and just. He was the king who would rule not for a temporary term like every other king—but for eternity.

To this day, Jesus still rules with wisdom and justice. Although He died, Jesus' resurrection from the grave allowed him to conquer death. Therefore, His kingship will never die. You cannot make Jesus the King of your life—He already is King. Because of that, your goal is just like that of a loyal knight: to honor and worship the King with the ways that you act, think, and speak.

What talents and abilities do you have that would make you a good king?

_____

_____

Everyone is tempted to be his or her own sovereign ruler. How do you currently try to play that role in your life?

_____

_____

Write down the characteristics of Jesus that you think make him such a great king.

_____

_____

Have you surrendered your life to serve King Jesus? Write a short prayer to Jesus, telling Him you are His servant. Surrender anything in your life that has come between you and Him.

Verse 4

For to us a child is born, to us a son is given, and the
government will be on his shoulders. And he will be
called Wonderful Counselor, Mighty God, Everlasting Father, Prince of Peace.

—Isaiah 9:6

Have you seen *The Lion King*? The opening scene is mag-
nificent, especially when Rafiki holds Simba high above
his head for all the animals in the kingdom to see. They had
been awaiting the birth announcement of the king's son, and,
at last, it was here. The whole kingdom rejoiced when the son
was presented to them. There is just something about the
fever pitch of hope and excitement in that scene that makes
you want to hold your cat high in the air for all the neighborhood pets to see.

The birth announcement for Jesus came several hundred
years before he was actually born. That alone shows that
this was not your typical "It's a Boy!" announcement. Read
Isaiah 9:6–7. This passage says that the entire government
will rest on the shoulders of this child and that his reign will
never end. He is better than any king before or after—even
the beloved and revered King David. Who could fulfill this role
of being called Wonderful Counselor, Mighty God, Everlasting

Father, and Prince of Peace? As the years passed, some of the Israelites lost hope that they would ever get a king like this. But we know from Scripture that the Israelites' prayers were answered in an incredible way. A Messiah did come. Jesus, God's Son, fulfilled every prophecy ever written.

"So," you ask, "what does that mean for me today?" Good question. First, you can know that God is faithful to keep His promises. He promised Jesus. He delivered Jesus. God keeps all His promises. You can count on Him. Second, Jesus is just who Isaiah said He would be. Jesus is everlasting. He will not leave you. Jesus is mighty. He is powerful enough to handle all your doubts and fears. Jesus brings peace. He can bring peace to your soul. And a day is coming when He will bring peace to this world. For good.

Will you be ready when He comes?

How has Jesus made a difference in your life? Think about some real and practical ways that your life has changed because of Him.

_____

_____

Do you turn to Jesus for help and guidance? If so, what have been the results? If not, what is keeping you from doing so?

_____

_____

Do you know people who need the peace and rest that only Jesus can bring? Pray for them now that they will give their needs, fears, desires, and plans over to Christ.

_____

_____

Verse 5

I and the Father are one.

—John 10:30

Family reunions are bittersweet to me. On the one hand, I can't stand it when people tell me that they remember when I was in diapers and when I used to make table art with my peanut butter. On the other hand, I love it when people tell me I look like my dad. As I grew up, I thought it was cool when people would mistake my voice for my dad's on the phone. One day, after my dad ate lunch with me at my high school, some of my friends came up to me and said, "I couldn't tell the difference between you and your dad when he was here." I considered it an honor to be mistaken for my dad.

Read John 10:22–30. The Jews were angry with Jesus in this passage. They claimed He would not tell them whether He was the Christ. Jesus, however, answered their question when He told them He was doing miracles in His Father's name. Jesus went on to say that He and His Father are one. The things His Father did, He did. The things His Father said, He said. Jesus claimed that if His Father was doing a miracle, it was Jesus doing the miracle. How could this be? It was because Jesus and His Father are one. The Father and Jesus do not merely resemble each other like I resemble my father—Jesus said, "I and the Father are one."

If people want to know God, they have to get to know Jesus. People cannot know God without knowing Jesus. When you read what Jesus said and pay attention to how He treated people, you're actually getting to know God as well. It's amazing that we can know so much about God by looking at Jesus and His life.

Think about the people whom you'd like to be mistaken for. What about them do you want to look like?

_____

_____

_____

_____

Make a list of three people whom your friends say you resemble in attitude or personality. Why do you "look" like them?

_____

_____

_____

_____

If your best friends made a list of the things you do or say that resemble Jesus, what would they say? What would your mom say? How about the person you have a crush on?

_____

_____

_____

_____

Verse 6

The Word became flesh and made his dwelling among us. We have seen his glory, the glory of the One and only Son, who came from the Father, full of grace and truth.

—John 1:14

Road trips are cool. The best part? You get to see lots of places in a short amount of time. We often take road trips to places we want to visit but probably would never live in. These places may be great to visit for whatever reason, but you wouldn't necessarily want to call them home. It's not like you'd be in a hurry to leave your friends, school, and family to move there.

Read John 1:1–14. This passage speaks about the Word being in the beginning with God. But John doesn't stop there. John says that not only was the Word with God, but the Word *was* God. What (or who) did John mean when he referred to the Word? This is a reference to Jesus. Jesus was with God in the beginning because Jesus is God.

Verse 14 says that the Word became flesh and dwelled among us. You may have heard of the really churchy phrase: *Word incarnate*. What this means is that the Word, Jesus, became "flesh" the moment He was born here on earth. Jesus was no longer far away. He was here with real skin and bones, breathing oxygen just like you and me.

The most important part of this passage is the fact that Jesus came to live with us. We do not worship some made-up figure that cannot relate to us. Jesus did not just come and visit us on some heavenly road-trip. He came to do life here with us. He was not simply passing through. He lived, ate, slept, laughed, cried, died, and was even raised from the dead here.

There is nothing you have experienced here on earth that Jesus didn't experience. He can relate to you in so many ways because He's been where you are.

Sometimes it's easy to feel like Jesus is far away and doesn't understand what you're going through. What are you struggling with that you feel Jesus can't relate to?

_____

_____

_____

How does it make you feel to know that Jesus lived a human life with all the same needs and feelings you have? How does that help you know that He can relate to you?

_____

_____

_____

What's keeping you from telling Jesus how you're feeling and what you're thinking?

_____

_____

Verse 7

Then those who were in the boat worshiped him, saying, "Truly you are the Son of God."

—Matthew 14:33

Think back to the Christian camps or retreats you've attended. You probably felt really close to God while you were there. That's an awesome feeling, isn't it? The problem is that it's easy for your spiritual high to last a short time and then … go back to normal. Am I right? You might be surprised, but Jesus' disciples struggled with this as well.

Read Matthew 14:22–33. This must have been one of the coolest days for a disciple of Jesus. First, they witnessed Jesus feeding thousands of people with only a little food. A few hours later, they saw Jesus walking on water. However, between the first miracle and the second one, they doubted Jesus was God's Son. The Bible says as Jesus was walking on the water, the disciples thought He was a ghost. Only after Peter tried out his sea legs did they recognize Jesus. When Peter sank and Jesus brought him back to the boat, the other disciples declared Jesus must really be the Son of God. What happened between the miraculous feeding of the thousands and Jesus' water-walk to change their minds? Why did they doubt?

We do the same thing. Why is it so hard for us to keep that spiritual high between camps or retreats? Maybe it is not just camps. It might be Sunday to Sunday or Sunday to Wednesday … Peter teaches us how to believe in those times. He trusted that Jesus would let him walk on water and that Jesus would save him if he sank. Peter obeyed Jesus when he was told to walk on water. Peter proclaimed Jesus as God's Son with his actions. The others did it with their lips.

Talk is cheap and easily fades away. How do your actions demonstrate to the world your faith in Christ?

In your own words, why do you think it is so challenging to keep your faith strong between the spiritual high points of your life?

_____

_____

Write down three specific ways in which you can declare to the world around you today through your actions and words that you believe Jesus is the Son of God.

_____

_____

Pray that your faith would be strengthened through the power of the Holy Spirit. Ask the Spirit to lead you into a deeper relationship with God today and to keep you solid through the low points in your life.

_____

_____

Verse 8

"Go away! What do you want with us, Jesus of Naz-
areth? Have you come to destroy us? I know who
you are—the Holy One of God!"

—Luke 4:34

On July 6, 2008, what most experts have called the greatest tennis match in history was played at Wimbledon. If
you're not a tennis fan, you need to know that Wimbledon is
the sport's largest event. In that contest, the two biggest stars
in men's tennis battled out in a slugfest for the ages. To end
the longest finals match in the sport's history, the underdog,
Spain's Rafael Nadal, beat the favorite, Switzerland's Roger
Federer. It was arguably one of the greatest sporting events
in history.

Rather than trash his opponent when the match was over,
Federer was gracious and full of praise in defeat. "[Nadal] is a
deserving champion," Federer said. "He just played fantasti-
cally." Isn't it interesting that an opponent would acknowledge
the greatness of the individual who had defeated him?

Read Luke 4:31–37. In this passage, a demon-possessed
man met Jesus. The demon cried out that Jesus was the Holy
One of God. Jesus was so powerful that the demon had to
acknowledge Jesus as divine and submit to His commands. It's
interesting that even after the demons proclaimed Jesus as

holy, the people listening were still unsure as to where Jesus had received His authority. What does that say about the people in the synagogue?

Sometimes it is hard for us to fully comprehend who Jesus really is—the holy Son of God. But Jesus' enemies know exactly who He is! Here's the truth: There is no demonic power that Jesus hasn't overcome. And if Jesus' enemies recognize His power, shouldn't we? If those whom Jesus has completely defeated acknowledge His greatness, shouldn't we (the ones He has saved) do the same?

Demons submit to Jesus because of who He is. Do you?

Describe a time in the past when you found it hard to trust that Jesus has the power to direct your life and the world around you.

_____

_____

_____

How does Jesus remind you that He is powerful, holy, and divine?

_____

_____

_____

What areas of fear in your life do you need to submit to Jesus' power?

_____

_____

_____

Verse 9

The men were amazed and asked, "What kind of man is this? Even the winds and the waves obey him!"

—Matthew 8:27

When I was younger, I loved to play outside. I played every day during the summer. But my mom wouldn't let me go outside when it rained. Whenever that happened, I would sing a little song to try to make it stop raining: "Rain, rain go away, come again another day ..." It seems a little silly now, but I thought it would work when I was a kid. The problem was that it never worked. No matter how hard I tried to stop the rain, I didn't have the power to do it.

Matthew 8 tells a story of Jesus and His disciples in a boat. Suddenly, a storm came upon them, and the disciples were terrified. Jesus asked why they were afraid (even though He knew they were freaking out because of the storm). Jesus knew they didn't fully understand that He was the one who had created the wind and rain. Unlike my powerless singing as a kid, when Jesus told the wind and rain to stop—they listened. Look at Matthew 8:23–27 to read the story for yourself.

Nothing surprises God. Not storms, not earthquakes ... nothing. We are the only ones caught off guard. The winds obey Jesus and submit to His authority. And just like the winds, we are to submit as well. See, God wants us to trust in Him and in His Son, Jesus. That is what the disciples did. In the middle of the storm, they cried out, "Lord, save us." They believed in God's power to save them.

We have seen in recent years how people come together after hurricanes and other disasters. Christians, churches, and youth groups come together to love people and turn to God for comfort during their distress. God wants us to trust Him even in the midst of storms.

Why should we trust God? Because He is always in control. Always.

Have there been times in your life when you turned to Jesus and He provided you a way out of a trying situation? Write down a short summary of what happened.

_____

_____

_____

How did Jesus' demonstration of His authority in this situation help you to draw closer to Him?

_____

_____

_____

Write a prayer to Jesus that thanks Him for being active in your life. Praise Jesus for His power and authority and for His willingness to use it for the good of His children.

_____

_____

Verse 10

He is before all things, and in him all things hold together.

—Colossians 1:17

D o you enjoy video games? Many people love not only the excitement of the games but also the feeling of being in complete control. And being in control is awesome.

Read Colossians 1:15–20. Jesus has real control. As the Son of God, Jesus has power and authority over the created world (and everything in it, including power over death and sin). But one of the coolest aspects of Jesus' role as the Son is that He quite literally keeps all of creation going. How do we know this? It's that little phrase in verse 17: "in him all things hold together."

The word *sustain* means to hold things together and strengthen. The whole universe is sustained, held together, kept going, and made stronger by Jesus. That is serious control!

Jesus' power is real. He does not simply hold a controller. He *is* the controller. Not only does He have the power to control all things, but through His power Jesus holds all things together. Jesus' role as sustainer is an amazing comfort in our lives. You can be confident that no matter what happens in the world, Jesus is keeping everything together and moving

toward a future that He has set in motion. Nothing is a surprise to Him. Jesus is in control.

Rest easy. Jesus is in control.

Do you ever worry about your future? Or the future of the
world around you? (It's OK if you do—it's natural.) If so, how
does knowing that Jesus holds everything together change the
way you feel?

_____

_____

_____

_____

_____

What areas of your life do you need to trust to Jesus' control?

_____

_____

_____

_____

_____

How can you trust the really personal things in your life to
Jesus' control more consistently?

_____

_____

_____

_____

_____

Verse 11

Jesus answered, "I am the way and the truth and the life. No one comes to the Father except through me."

—John 14:6

Those of you who have a license to drive can relate to what I'm about to write. (If you don't have your license yet, then I'm sorry to rub it in.) There are several signs that you have to learn for your driving test, right? But there are two big ones you'll want to remember. The first is the "One Way" sign and the other is the "Wrong Way" sign. "One Way" signs are black with white letters and point in one direction. When you see this sign, you want to make sure you follow the direction of the arrow. However, if you make a wrong turn down a one-way street, you'll see another sign. It's big and red with "Wrong Way" printed on it. These signs serve as warnings because you are in danger of hitting another car. Trust me. I know from experience. You don't want to see the "Wrong Way" sign.

Read what Jesus says in John 14:1–7. In our passage for today, Jesus is telling His disciples about heaven and that they already know how to get there. But one of them says to Jesus, "We don't know the way." Jesus replies, "I am the way." If we know Jesus, then we know the way to heaven. Jesus is literally the only way to get there. He is not *a* way. He is the "One Way." All other ways amount to the "Wrong Way."

If there was an actual road sign to heaven, it would be a "One Way" sign pointing to Jesus. If you were to turn away from Christ, then you would see "Wrong Way" signs warning you that danger is ahead. There would be "Wrong Way" signs on the road of "doing all the right things" or "going to church all the time." The only way to get to heaven is the "One Way" found in faith in Jesus Christ. All other roads lead to dangerous lifestyles and eternal separation from God.

Which way are you headed?

What are some popular beliefs in the world today about how to get to heaven?

_____

_____

What do you think it takes to get to heaven?

_____

_____

If you are unsure of whether you are on the right road, take some time to talk to an adult in your church. Express your concerns to him or her. In the meantime, take a moment to write a prayer to God that expresses your fears and concerns. Ask Him to confirm for you that He truly is the pathway to eternal life.

_____

_____

Verse 12

In your relationships with one another, have the same mindset as Christ Jesus

—Philippians 2:5

Have you ever heard a guy referred to as "a real man"? Does this mean that he used to be made out of wood and then came to life like Pinocchio? All kidding aside, people use that phrase to refer to their ideal picture of a man. It implies a standard for manhood that's usually associated with toughness, strength, etc. You probably have an image of what you see as an ideal person. This was true for people in Jesus' time too.

The Jews anticipated the Messiah, God's Son, with great expectation. Many of them envisioned the Messiah coming with political power to rule an earthly kingdom. God had different plans, though. He chose to send Jesus to earth in the form of a helpless child who would grow to be a rabbi to a group of fishermen and tax collectors. Jesus, God in the flesh, ruled in heaven and sat on His throne as King of the universe. But He gave everything up to become a servant. In that moment, He became a real man—the ideal man.

Read Philippians 2:5–7. Paul, the writer of Philippians, teaches us a great lesson in this passage. He says we should have the same attitude of humility that Jesus had. If there was anyone who deserved to be treated like a king, it was Jesus. He came to earth, however, to serve. Jesus' life teaches us the power of love and humility.

When we succeed and people applaud us, more times than not we start feeling important. This creates a problem. When we think we are important, we simultaneously think other people are less important. That is why Paul's message is so vital for us. If the King of the universe put others' needs before His own safety and comfort, what can we ever achieve that would lead us to think that we are more important than others?

Our attitude should be that of humility ... just like Christ.

1.Compare your attitude to what you know (and to what Paul says) about Jesus' attitude. Does your attitude imitate Jesus' attitude?

_____

_____

_____

2.What changes do you need to make in your attitude for it to become more like Christ's?

_____

_____

_____

3.How can you show humility even if you feel important?

_____

_____

Verse 13

"For even the Son of Man did not come to be served, but to serve, and to give his life as a ransom for many."

—Mark 10:45

During your next trip to the movies, try this experiment. Wait until you see a really big dude get in line. Then go cut right in front of him. When he taps you on the shoulder (which he definitely will) and tells you to get back to your original spot in line, tell him that you are more important than he is and that he needs to let you go in front of him. If you're lucky enough to wake up after he's done responding to you with his big fists, please tell me how this experiment worked out.

People naturally want their needs met before the needs of others. We think we are more important than our neighbor. That's the reason the big dude in the movie ticket line would be so unhappy with you for breaking the line. In his mind, his needs come before yours. But God calls us to reverse this trend.

Take a look at Mark 10:35–45. In this passage, two of the disciples asked Jesus for a favor. Basically, they wanted to be highly regarded in heaven. Jesus, however, had some very sobering words for them. He said that the officials of their day used (and probably often abused) their authority over people.

Jesus then told them that He did not come to earth to be served but to serve. Jesus knew that service is a hard concept for people to understand, so He came as a servant to show us how to serve.

The way we can become better Christians is to work on the way in which we serve others. Just as the disciples were expected to put others first, so are we. We are not supposed to be Christians that expect a pat on the back all the time. Christians should serve other people. There is a responsibility that comes with the privilege of being a Christian. This responsibility is to serve others.

On a scale of one to ten (with ten representing the best), how would you rate yourself as a servant?

_____

_____

_____

_____

What are some ways in which you can serve others?

_____

_____

_____

_____

What areas of service do you need to work on?

_____

_____

_____

_____

Verse 14

"Which is easier: to say, 'Your sins are forgiven,' or
to say, 'Get up and walk'?"

—Luke 5:23

Have you ever done something you thought was private,
but it really wasn't? Steve Carell, as Maxwell Smart,
encountered this in the movie *Get Smart*. CONTROL told Smart
that they were making him a field agent. Not wanting to show
the others how excited he was, he chose to celebrate where
no one could hear him—in the Cone of Silence. The Cone of
Silence is an invisible chamber inside which, when activated,
no one can hear your conversation. Thinking that the other
people couldn't hear him, Smart started yelling in jubilee
about the news. There was only one problem: he hadn't activated the Cone properly, so everyone could hear him yelling.

The Pharisees in our passage obviously thought they were
in the Cone of Silence around Jesus. The Teacher, however,
heard their thoughts.

Read Luke 5:17–26. By the time these guys brought their
friend to meet the Savior, Jesus had healed many people. The
crowd had witnessed many miracles up to that point, but they
didn't expect to hear what they heard next. The Bible says
that when Jesus saw their faith, he told the man that his sins
were forgiven. Jesus knew the Pharisees doubted his ability to

forgive sins. They hated Jesus and were always causing trouble. Do you think they were shocked when Jesus turned to them and told them what they were thinking? Jesus not only heard their thoughts, but he knew their hearts as well.

Sometimes we think Jesus doesn't know what we are thinking because we do things in private. Jesus, however, knows our thoughts and the condition of our heart. Even if we hide things from people, we cannot hide our thoughts from Jesus. We might be able to trick people into thinking we are good Christians by going to church or wearing Christian t-shirts. But we cannot trick Jesus. He knows the hearts and the motives of everyone.

Describe a time when you thought that you were doing something privately, only to find out that it wasn't so private. How did it make you feel when you realized that you were exposed?

_____

_____

_____

What thoughts would you be ashamed for other people to know?

_____

_____

_____

How does it make you feel that Jesus knows your thoughts—even the bad ones?

_____

_____

Verse 15

Jesus wept.

—John 11:35

Has this ever happened to you? Someone says, "I can relate to what you're going through," but you know that they really can't. I would rather someone plainly tell me that they have no idea what I'm going through than to tell me they can relate when they really can't. The death of a loved one is something that most people can relate to. However, until you've experienced the pain that comes with losing someone close to you, you really don't know how bad it hurts. Jesus knows how to relate to us because He lost someone very dear to him.

Read John 11:17–37. Pay close attention to verses 33–37. During Jesus' life, He built many relationships, but He was especially close to the family of Mary, Martha, and Lazarus. When Jesus learned Lazarus was sick, He purposefully did not come to make him better. Of course, Jesus could have kept him from dying, but He didn't. He allowed Lazarus to die so that the people could see Jesus' power over death. Although Jesus knew He would raise Lazarus from the dead, he also knew the seriousness of death. Jesus saw the pain that Mary and Martha felt, and He hurt with them. The Bible says, "Jesus wept." Jesus truly hurt because of his friend's death.

Jesus can relate to you when you experience pain of any sort. He comforts you when you hurt. Jesus wept with Mary and Martha. He genuinely cares for you and knows the pain you feel. Even if you think no one knows what you are going through when you are hurting, Jesus knows how you feel. You can trust Him and turn to Him in your pain.

Jesus can comfort you because He has been there.

How did you feel when you read verses 33–37?

_____

_____

_____

How does it make you feel to know that Jesus offers comfort when you are feeling pain or a deep sense of loss?

_____

_____

_____

_____

Are you hurting? Are you fearful about something? Do you feel lost or depressed? Has your heart been broken? Turn to Jesus right now and ask Him to ease your pain. Write the following statement in the space below: "Jesus, I believe you can take my pain away. While I wait for that to happen, I trust you to comfort me too."

_____

_____

_____

_____

Verse 16

Jesus answered, "It is written: 'Man shall not live on bread alone.'"

—Luke 4:4

There is a video circulating on the Internet that you might have seen. The clip, taken on a safari in Kruger, Africa, shows a herd of water buffalo at a watering hole. The buffalo do not see the nearby lions lurking in the grass. When the herd approaches the oasis, the lions attack. They do not attack the biggest buffalo, rather, they attack the weakest member of the group—the most vulnerable one. After a series of amazing events among the lions, buffalo, and crocodiles, the baby buffalo escapes. He did not, however, escape on his own. The herd joined forces and attacked the lions on behalf of the baby. Alone, the baby buffalo was helpless, but with the group, he was saved.

1 Peter 5:8–9 says that the devil prowls around like a roaring lion looking for someone to devour. Although he will attack, we can resist him and escape his schemes. Jesus taught us how to resist him because Satan tempted Jesus too.

Read Luke 4:1–13. Satan used interesting tactics when tempting Jesus. He attacked Jesus where he thought He was most vulnerable. Jesus was hungry, and Satan tempted Him with food. Jesus had given up His place in heaven for life on earth, so Satan tempted Him with power and the promise of many kingdoms. If Jesus had simply asked the angels, they would have rescued Him, so Satan tempted Him with their obedience. The only counterattack that Jesus used was quoting Scripture to Satan. Simple, but effective.

Satan will often tempt you at your weakest point in life. He will find where you are most vulnerable and attack you. Although you may stumble, you can resist Satan the same way Jesus did. Satan has no power over God's Word. Jesus was tempted, but He prevailed. He will help you prevail too.

Identify the weakest parts of your life and the areas in which Satan attacks you.

_____

_____

_____

_____

Write down three Bible verses that can help you in these areas.

_____

_____

_____

_____

Describe a situation in which you used a memory verse to help you resist temptation.

_____

_____

_____

_____

Verse 17

"Why were you searching for me?" he asked. "Didn't you know I had to be in my Father's house?"

—Luke 2:49

Would you say you have changed a lot since you were young? The answer seems pretty straightforward. But in some cases, you're a lot like the person today you were growing up. Many people in high school like the same things they liked in junior high. And many people in college have the same likes and dislikes they had in high school.

The same goes for your spiritual life. If you develop good Bible study habits when you are young, they stay with you as you age. This was also true for Jesus. His ministry didn't start when He was an adult. He laid the foundation when He was a young boy.

Read Luke 2:41–52. Jesus and his parents would go every year to Jerusalem for the Feast of the Passover. This particular time, however, Jesus chose to stay at the temple and question the religious leaders. The leaders couldn't understand how He knew so much about the Scriptures. The reason Jesus knew so much about Scripture was because He inspired the writings of the Scriptures. In fact, Jesus is the one about whom the Scriptures are written.

Although Jesus' public ministry began when he was about thirty years old, He didn't wait until then to start preparing. It's not like he crammed all night before He performed His first miracle. Jesus prepared His whole life for the plan God had for Him. Similarly, you and I should start preparing now for the plan God has for us.

The way we live our life now and how seriously we take our relationship with Christ will determine how we live tomorrow.

What are some good habits you have now that you want to continue as you get older?

_____

_____

_____

_____

What are some not-so-good habits you'd like to stop before you get older?

_____

_____

_____

_____

Write two or three spiritual goals that you would like to accomplish during the next week, month, and year.

_____

_____

_____

_____

Verse 18

God made him who had no sin to be sin for us, so that in him we might become the righteousness of God.

—2 Corinthians 5:21

One of my hobbies is woodcarving. I carve little figurines and turn them into Christmas ornaments for friends. I start with a plain block of wood and then begin carving with a knife. When I start carving, I know exactly what I want the figurine to look like. Sometimes I cut big chunks and other times I make small, intricate cuts. The process from beginning to end is time-consuming, but the result is very fulfilling.

Now it's time for a vocabulary lesson. Have you ever heard the word *justification*? This term means showing something is right or reasonable—or not guilty. What about the word *righteousness*? This word deals with God's way of making people right in His own eyes. Finally, what about *sanctification*? This is the process of becoming more like who Jesus wants you to be.

Now, with these definitions in mind, stop and read 2 Corinthians 5:21. Here is how it works. God has justified us (declared us as "not guilty") through Jesus' death on the cross and resurrection from the grave. We are made righteous (right in God's eyes) through sanctification (the process of becoming who Jesus wants us to be).

A woodcarver was asked the question, "How do you carve an eagle?" He replied, "It's easy. You take this block of wood and cut away anything that doesn't look like an eagle." Sanctification is very similar to a block of wood in a master carver's hand. The carver chooses the wood and then makes it into a masterpiece. He looks past the formless block of wood and sees the wonderful end result. Sometimes the process is painful and takes a long time, but eventually the block becomes a masterpiece.

Since you have been made "not guilty," God wants to make you into the person you should be.

How does it feel to know that God is shaping you into a masterpiece?

_____

_____

_____

In what area of your life is God carving away big chunks to make you look more like Him? What are the small intricate cuts that He's making?

_____

_____

_____

Take the three vocabulary words from today and define them in your own words. Write down what they personally mean to you. Then read them to God as a prayer of thanksgiving.

_____

_____

Verse 19

But he was pierced for our transgressions, he was crushed for our iniquities; the punishment that brought us peace was upon him, and by his wounds we are healed.

—Isaiah 53:5

There was an article in a California newspaper several years ago about a sixteen-year-old girl who had just received her driver's license. She was driving by herself, enjoying the freedom of the open road, when she lost track of her speed. As she topped a hill, she saw red and blue lights flashing in her rearview mirror. The policeman pulled her over and gave her a speeding ticket. Wanting to appeal the ticket in court, she showed up and was denied by the judge and was deemed guilty as charged. He issued her a fine of several hundred dollars for the price of the ticket. What makes this story unique is that after issuing the fine, the judge stepped off the bench. He removed his robe, pulled out his wallet, and paid the fine. The judge was the girl's father, and he paid the price of the ticket for her.

Read Isaiah 53:1–5. Try something different today by reading this Scripture out loud. Sometimes it helps to hear or see things in a fresh way when we do something besides what we're accustomed to doing.

The price of sin costs much more than a speeding ticket. Paul tells us in Romans 6:23 that the price of sin is death, but the gift of God is eternal life in Christ Jesus. We are all guilty as charged in our sin, but Jesus paid the price for us by dying on the cross. Our passage from Isaiah today prophesied Jesus' death. God gave these words to the prophet Isaiah so that the world would expect a Savior. Jesus was that Savior.

Each of us deserves the kind of punishment Jesus endured. We are the guilty ones, but Jesus took our place on the cross as payment for our sinful nature. Therefore, we should always remember Isaiah's words. We have peace and eternal life because of the punishment that Jesus received.

Think about a time when someone took your place and was punished instead of you. How did it make you feel? How did your attitude toward that person change after they did that for you?

_____

_____

How does it make you feel that it was Jesus who died on the cross instead of you?

_____

_____

What are some of the daily things you do that reflect the way you feel toward Jesus' selfless act of love?

_____

_____

_____

Verse 20

While they were eating, Jesus took bread, and when he had given thanks, he broke it and gave it to his disciples, saying, "Take it; this is my body."

—Mark 14:22

I have always loved Thanksgiving, but after I got married, I think my love for this holiday bumped up a notch. See, for years I only had one Thanksgiving meal at Thanksgiving. But since I've been married, I have two every Thanksgiving. How awesome is that? Two turkeys, two sweet potato pies, and two tubs of dressing make me salivate every time. I do love the food. But even more than that, I love the thought of gathering around a table with family and friends to enjoy a meal together. Some of my fondest memories as a child are from Thanksgiving with my grandparents around a dinner table. Those times were special. As I read today's passage, I wonder if Jesus felt the same way.

Read Mark 14:22–26. Jesus was speaking metaphorically when He told His disciples that the bread was His body and the wine was His blood. Jesus knew that the coming night would be special because it was His last night before being crucified. He wanted His disciples to remember that night, so He gave them something to remember Him by—the food they ate. Wine and bread were common at meals in Jesus' time. Yet

He chose those ordinary items to represent His extraordinary sacrifice so that every time they ate bread and drank wine, they would remember what Jesus had done for them.

When we say the blessing or give thanks before a meal, it should involve more than thanking God for the food we are about to eat. We should remember the sacrifice Jesus made for us on the cross. Just as eating is something we never forget to do, neither should we forget what Jesus did for us. So, next time you sit down to a meal and say the blessing, remember to thank Jesus for giving Himself for you just like He provided the food before you.

What are some of your favorite Thanksgiving foods?

_____

_____

_____

_____

What good memories have you shared with friends and family around the dinner table?

_____

_____

_____

_____

Write down five reasons for why you are thankful for Jesus.

_____

_____

_____

_____

Verse 21

When he had received the drink, Jesus said, "It is finished." With that, he bowed his head and gave up his spirit.

—John 19:30

Let's play a little game. I am going to give you a list, and you should respond by telling me what they have in common. Here we go:

- your elementary school years
- President George W. Bush's term
- the year 2003
- dinosaurs
- the Ice Age

Do you have any idea? Here's the answer: These things are all finished. They have been completed, and nothing more can be added to them.

Read John 19:28—30. John 19 is all about Jesus on the cross and how His earthly ministry has come to an end. Jesus' goal while on earth was to restore people to God. The only way to accomplish this was for Jesus to take on the sins of the world.

The catch was that Jesus had to die when He took on this burden because the penalty of sin is death.

My favorite part of John 19:30 is that Jesus "gave up" His spirit. No one took Jesus' life—He gave it up. He was obedient to the purpose His Father had sent Him to accomplish. He was obedient even to death. This act of obedience completed the work He set out to finish. While on the cross, Jesus proclaimed His work was finished. This phrase, "It is finished," is the most comforting thing Jesus could have said on the cross. This phrase gives us life and access to God.

Jesus had to die. Although He knew it would be an agonizing process, He remained obedient and looked past the process to see the end result. Sometimes the process is hard and not much fun while we are in the middle of it, but finishing something is always a good feeling. Jesus knew if He quit before He finished you and I would have no hope of salvation.

Following Jesus is going to be hard but being obedient is worth it.

What accomplishment are you most proud of?

_____

_____

Why is following Jesus difficult at times?

_____

_____

When have you been obedient to Jesus and rewarded at the end?

_____

_____

Verse 22

For we do not have a high priest who is unable to empathize with our weaknesses, but we have one who has been tempted in every way, just as we are—yet he did not sin.

—Hebrews 4:15

Counterfeit money has always intrigued me. Don't worry. I don't have any and have never possessed any. (Not that I know of, at least.) Yet, it is still an interesting concept to me. This is how I understand it: You want to buy something, so you take real money, make a copy of the real thing, and try to pay for whatever you originally wanted. I've never really understood how people get away with doing this, but I know that it happens all the time. It's funny to me that no matter how close to the real thing counterfeit money may appear, it's still a copy. It's worthless unless you want to start a fire or take on a papier-mâché project.

For our sin to be covered, someone had to fulfill the Law. Not just some of it—all of it. Read Hebrews 4:15. Until Jesus came, no one had ever kept the entire Law. People didn't even come close. Even though they tried to keep the Law, the very fact that they were born into sin kept them from being sinless. Jesus, however, was faced with the same temptations you and I are faced with, yet He remained sinless.

Until Jesus came, it was like people were using counter-feit money to pay the penalty that the Law demanded. When Jesus came, He was the only one worthy of paying the price that would fulfill the Law because He was the only one who upheld the Law. Jesus did not come to do away with the Law; He came to fulfill it so that the price could be paid for our sins.

Are you trying to pay for your sins with counterfeit money? Attempting to pay the price of your sins with anything other than Jesus' sacrifice is a waste of time. Jesus is the only "real thing."

What are some ways that people try to pay for their sins?

_____

_____

_____

_____

How does it make you feel to know that Jesus was faced with the same temptations as you?

_____

_____

_____

_____

How does your view of Jesus change now that you know Jesus was tempted too?

_____

_____

_____

_____

Verse 23

You see, at just the right time, when we were still powerless, Christ died for the ungodly.

—Romans 5:6

There's a famous story that goes like this: There was a man who did not believe that Jesus had died for his sins. He could not understand why God would send His Son to die for people who did not deserve it. While he was at home one day, it began snowing. The storm became a blizzard. Staring out his window, he noticed two birds caught in the storm. He could see that they were trying to escape into his nearby barn, but they kept flying into the window. He knew they would surely die if they stayed out in the snow, so he went outside to shoo the birds into the barn. But they flew away. He opened the window so that they could get out of the cold, but as he watched from inside, they still flew into the glass. He thought, "Those stupid birds could die out there. If only I could become a bird, I could lead them to safety." Right then and there he understood exactly why God had sent Jesus to die for the world.

We are powerless on our own. Jesus had to lead us to safety. Read Romans 5:6–8. There are not two roads to heaven: one for good people and one for those who trust in Jesus. Jesus didn't come as an alternative route of salvation for people who were not good enough to get to heaven. He died for all of us because none of us are good enough. Ephesians 2:8–9 says that we are saved by grace and not by works. Christ died for the ungodly. Sorry to tell you, but that includes you and me.

So, when you don't feel good enough to be a Christian, cheer up! You never were good enough—that's why Jesus died for you. And now you live in the freedom that comes from God's grace.

When do you feel most like a Christian?

_____

_____

_____

_____

How can you change the way that you feel during the times when you don't feel good enough to be a Christian?

_____

_____

_____

_____

Write down three to five ways to remind yourself that God loves you even though you are not good enough for salvation.

_____

_____

_____

_____

_____

Verse 24

For I am not ashamed of the gospel, because it is the power of God that brings salvation to everyone who believes: first to the Jew, then to the Gentile.

—Romans 1:16

I am from the South, where college football is king. Everywhere you go, seven days a week, people wear their team's colors to show their undying support. Every Saturday in the fall, literally millions of people travel hundreds of miles to their team's stadium. On Saturdays in the South, elementary schoolteachers paint their faces like crazed warriors, and preachers yell, "Hit him!" and grandparents curse as part of their favorite cheer. Yet nobody seems to think this behavior is odd. Here in the South, we unashamedly support our team. Sundays, however, are different. On Sundays, sometimes we don't even get out of bed for church—and if we do, it is often the first time that week that we've opened our Bible. It seems to me that many people are bigger football fans than they are followers of Jesus.

Does it sometimes feel as if people are ashamed of Jesus?

Read Romans 1:16. Paul was the furthest thing from ashamed. He recognized the importance and power of Christ's gospel and let everyone know his support for it. He knew the gospel was for everyone, and he wanted everyone to accept it. Paul was the epitome of boldness for the gospel. Jesus was more than someone he visited on Sundays. Paul's life reflected his love for Jesus. Why? Because Jesus had saved him and turned his life completely around. He could never be the same after he met Jesus. Jesus was important to him.

I wish that I had Paul's boldness regarding the gospel. In fact, it is sad to say, but I wish I had my own excitement about the gospel as I do my Auburn Tigers.

Supporting a team is so exclusive—you're either for us or against us. Salvation, on the other hand, is for everyone. Jesus offers salvation to all who believe in him.

How do you show love for your favorite team?

_____

_____

_____

_____

How do you show the world your love of Jesus?

_____

_____

_____

_____

What are some ways in which your life can show that you are not ashamed of Christ's gospel?

_____

_____

_____

_____

Verse 25

You may ask me for anything in my name, and I will
do it.

—John 14:14

In the movie *P.S. I Love You*, the husband of Hilary Swank's
character dies. He knew he was going to die for a while, so
before he passed away he wrote her several letters. She was
supposed to read these letters after his death to help her deal
with his absence. Swank's character, depressed with the loss
of her spouse, felt like he was still around because of the letters. She felt like he was there because he told her things to
do and trips to take so that she could get on with her life. It's a
chick flick, but a neat story.

Read John 14:9–14. Jesus is comforting His disciples
because He is about to leave them. He tells them that although
He is going to be with His Father, He will still be with them in
spirit. Jesus reassured them that His power would not leave
them. Even though Jesus left earth, He gave them access to
Him in Heaven. Jesus allowed them to ask for anything in His
name and promised that He would give it to them. This statement was intended to prove that He was going to be where He
promised He would be—with the Father.

Jesus gives us the same access to God's power. I truly believe in the power of Jesus' name and that He gives us what we ask so that it will bring glory to God. I do not believe, however, that if I ask for a 1969 Z28 Camaro in Jesus' name that I will get it. Jesus knows I do not need it, and it wouldn't glorify God. Jesus was referring to the disciples' needs for ministry and the promise of power even in His absence. Jesus knows your needs, and He offers you His power in order to meet them.

When have you felt Jesus' power in your life?

_____

_____

_____

_____

Why is it sometimes hard for you to believe that you have access to Jesus' power?

_____

_____

_____

_____

List three practical ways that you can remind yourself that Jesus is still with you even though you cannot see Him.

_____

_____

_____

_____

Verse 26

Fixing our eyes on Jesus, the pioneer and perfecter of faith. For the joy set before him he endured the cross, scorning its shame, and sat down at the right hand of the throne of God.

—Hebrews 12:2

My wife and I grew up in towns with lakes. She water-skied, and I fished. Naturally, we both love being on the water. In fact, our first purchase as a married couple was a giant yellow kayak made for two. Nevertheless, whether fishing or skiing, one thing to remember when driving a boat is to watch where you are going. If you look to the left or right, you are going to steer the boat to that side. The best way to drive in a straight line is to keep your eyes fixed on something stationary, like a tree or a house or maybe even a tree house. The same is true for your Christian life. But instead of a tree house, we look to Jesus, who will never change. He will always be there to keep us on the right path.

Stop and read Hebrews 12:1–3. Verse 2 describes Jesus as the pioneer and perfecter of our faith. That means if we are to follow anything by faith it should be Jesus. Why? Because He not only created our faith, but Jesus also makes our faith perfect. Hebrews 11:1 says that when we have faith, we are certain of what we cannot see. What can we not see? Well, salvation, for one. But we have faith that Jesus gives us salvation. He makes our faith perfect because when we have Jesus, we have salvation. Without Him, we have no hope of salvation. But with Jesus, our faith is made perfect because He gives us salvation.

People put their faith in many different things: money, sports, fame, good works, other people, etc. We cannot depend on those things because they will all pass away. We must fix our eyes on Jesus because He is the only thing in this world on whom we can completely depend.

What things or people have let you down after you put your faith in them?

_____

_____

_____

_____

What are some ways you can keep your focus on Jesus instead of other things?

_____

_____

_____

_____

What are three things that can help you keep your focus on Jesus in the future? Who are three people who will help you?

_____

_____

_____

Verse 27

Whoever finds their life will lose it, and whoever loses their life for my sake will find it.

—Matthew 10:39

Jim Elliot, a missionary to Ecuador during the 1940s and 50s, was killed while ministering to the Huaorani people. After Elliot died, his wife, Elisabeth, returned to the Huaorani people and had incredible success with the gospel. Before Jim died, he wrote a famous quote in his journal that said, "He is no fool who gives what he cannot keep to gain that which he cannot lose." The story of Jim and the four other missionaries who died was fictionalized in a movie titled *End of the Spear*. Jim surrendered his life to Jesus and in return gained a life that was eternal.

Read Matthew 10:39. Jesus told His followers these words just before He sent them out into the mission field. Jesus wanted them to realize that following Him was more than just saying that they were His disciples. He wanted them to know the importance of completely surrendering their life to Him in ministry. He didn't want partially committed followers. Jesus wanted those who followed Him to be His lifelong disciples. His words reassured His followers that even if they gave up their life, they would find it in Jesus. If they searched for their own life outside of Jesus, however, they would lose it.

Life outside of Christ is death. Even though following Christ may cost you your life, you really receive life. If I live without Jesus, I die. If I live with Jesus, I must lose my life to be with him. Sounds confusing at times, but it's pretty simple.

Jesus wants us to be His lifelong disciples. He demands we give up our life, our plans, and our dreams in exchange for His life for us. You and I may not die on the mission field like Jim Elliot, but we must surrender our life to Christ to receive abundant life.

What sacrifices have you made in order to follow Jesus?

_____

_____

_____

_____

_____

What does it look like to "lose your life for Christ"?

_____

_____

_____

_____

_____

How can you lose your life for Christ and still live?

_____

_____

_____

_____

_____

Verse 28

Therefore go and make disciples of all nations, bap-
tizing them in the name of the Father and of the
Son and of the Holy Spirit.

—Matthew 28:19

Have you ever been on a mission trip? It's a pretty cool
experience, right? I've been on both national and international mission trips, and they are equally amazing when it
comes to seeing how God works. But I sometimes think we
have the idea that missions can only take place when we are
on trips. Missions are not limited to the remote places of the
world. You can be a missionary while flipping burgers at your
after-school job.

Read Matthew 28:16–20. This passage is known as the
Great Commission. But somewhere along the way, the focus
shifted away from what Jesus originally intended for His disciples. The action statement of "go and make disciples" can be
somewhat misleading because in the original Greek the only
verb in the phrase is what's translated as "make disciples." The
word *go* is actually a participle and can be translated as "in
your goings." If we read it according to how Jesus actually said
it, we shift our focus from where we do missions to how we
do missions.

Making disciples takes time and consistency. Jesus wants us to make disciples wherever we are and not just on trips. Whether at your school, on your team, in your band, at your job, in your home, neighborhood, college dorm room, or wherever you are—in your goings, make disciples.

How do you make a disciple? Look at Jesus' model. He devoted His life to His disciples. He spent time with them. He taught them the Scriptures. He ate with them, walked with them, spent the night at some of their houses, and prayed with them. He didn't just show up for a few days, read a verse or two from the Bible, sing a song, and then leave.

Jesus made disciples by devoting His life to His followers. That is what we are called to do as well: devote our life to the one we follow.

How can you make disciples wherever you go?

_____

_____

_____

Think of someone who has discipled you. Now write about what that was like. What did you do? How did it work? Did you meet weekly, monthly, or daily? Where did you meet together?

_____

_____

_____

How is disciple-making different from decision-making?

_____

_____

Verse 29

Jesus looked at him and loved him. "One thing you lack," he said. "Go, sell everything you have and give to the poor, and you will have treasure in heaven. Then come, follow me."

—Mark 10:21

As I write this book, our economy is sinking. People have lost billions of dollars. In a poor economy, everyone looks for safe investments, but there are no sure things. Risks are always involved. In fact, most investment disclaimers tell you that it is possible for you to actually lose your money. But in our passage for today, Jesus talks about a different kind of investing: that of investing your life.

Read Mark 10:17–31. Many times, people came to Jesus along the roads where He traveled and asked Him questions. This story tells about a rich young man who wanted to know how to receive eternal life. Jesus' answer shocked those listening. What?! Sell everything? And give it to who?! Why would Jesus ask him to do that? Because Jesus knew the man loved his earthly treasure more than his heavenly treasure.

In verses 28–31, Jesus says those who give up something to follow Jesus will receive a hundred times what they gave up. That is a great return on your investment. Most financial advisors tell you to "diversify your portfolio" (spread out your investments) in the hope of gaining ten to twelve percent over the lifetime of the investment. Jesus tells us to give up everything to receive a hundred times that much in return. Investing your life in Jesus is a sure thing.

This is not a prosperity gospel promising that God will make you rich. This verse tells us that the blessing might be "in the age to come," meaning in heaven. Many times, our blessing comes from giving rather than getting. God wants us to be obedient to Him and give ourselves to others. Whether it is money, time, or possessions that we give God, we cannot out-give Him. He will always bless you with more than you give.

What things are you holding onto like the rich young man that you need to give to God?

_____

_____

_____

Why do we withhold things when God promises to bless us for giving them away?

_____

_____

_____

Name three to five ways that you can give more of yourself to God through your possessions.

_____

_____

_____

_____

Verse 30

For I was hungry and you gave me something to eat, I was thirsty and you gave me something to drink, I was a stranger and you invited me in.

—Matthew 25:35

The movie *Valkyrie* was based on the true story of the conspiracy to assassinate Adolf Hitler. Dietrich Bonhoeffer, the German theologian, was executed because of his involvement in the Valkyrie conspiracy, but he was not mentioned in the movie. As a pastor, Bonhoeffer believed that for us to show God's love to others, we had to serve them. In his book, *A Testament to Freedom,* he wrote, "Possessions are not God's blessing and goodness, but the opportunities of service which God entrusts to us." To Bonhoeffer, merely telling about God's love and neglecting someone's physical needs was not enough. He believed in actively loving people with service as opposed to passively loving them with our words.

Read Matthew 25:31–46. Ouch! This verse makes me cringe when I think about the missed opportunities that I have had in my life to serve Jesus. This story teaches us that whenever we serve others, we serve Jesus. He also said that when we fail to serve those in need, we fail to serve Him. This should change the way we view people. When we view opportunities to help people in need as opportunities to serve Jesus, our attitude should drastically change.

How can we serve God without serving people? It's not like we can go out to the city streets and give God a blanket or a warm bowl of soup. Or is it? In fact, based on our passage, the best way to serve God is to serve people. Read Matthew 22:37–40. This is why loving God and loving people are so closely related. The way we love God is by loving people, and the way to show God's love is by serving others.

I hope we keep this in mind the next time we have opportunities to serve those in need.

How can you practically show God's love at home? What about at school?

_____

_____

_____

_____

What keeps you from serving people when you know they are in need?

_____

_____

_____

_____

What can you do to change the way you view people in need?

_____

_____

_____

Verse 31

I am the vine; you are the branches. If you remain
in me and I in you, you will bear much fruit; apart
from me you can do nothing.

—John 15:5

I love vineyards. My grandfather grew muscadines and passed the art of growing and pruning vines down to my dad. It intrigues me as to how grape juice, wine, and jam can be made from a single fruit that grows on a vine. It baffles me to consider the way you can train a vine and prune it in just the right way to produce the best fruit. I love the picture of God as the gardener who prunes something that grows wild like a vine and then produces something wonderful. God's final product is a fruitful vineyard. What a beautiful image of a life of intimacy with Christ!

Read John 15:1–8. Jesus used the image of a vineyard to illustrate how we are helpless without Him. In the same way that we cannot have salvation without Jesus, we also cannot live apart from Him once we are in Him. Our calling is "to abide" in Christ, which is another way of saying "to remain" in Him. Abiding in Christ means living in Christ. We are called to take up residence in Christ. I'm not talking about a take-off-your-shoes-and-stay-for-a-while kind of abiding, rather,

I'm talking about bring-in-the-U-Haul-because-we-are-here-to-stay kind of abiding.

When you believe in Christ, then you are a branch connected to the vine: Jesus. The purpose of abiding in Christ is so that He can produce fruit in you. An eternal fruit that will last. You cannot produce the fruit yourself. Your job is to be the branch and let Jesus, the vine, do the work. This is what it means to abide: to see yourself as the branch and to remain in the vine as He produces the fruit.

Consider the roles of the gardener, vine, and branch, then state in which role you usually see yourself. What is the difference between producing fruit and abiding in Christ?

_____

_____

_____

_____

What does an intimate life abiding in Jesus look like to you?

_____

_____

_____

_____

How do you interact with the world differently when you step into your role as the branch?

_____

_____

_____

_____

Closing

Wow! You made it. You've just done something that fewer and fewer people are doing these days: finishing something. A lot of people start out strong on projects, goals, and even books, but few people finish. Way to go!

If you ever feel unloved, think again. Jesus loves you. Jesus' whole life and the reason He stepped out of heaven onto earth was because of His love for you and me.

Hopefully, after reading this book, you know more about who Jesus is and what He did for you. It's pretty amazing stuff, huh? But Jesus doesn't want you to simply know about him. Jesus wants you to have a relationship with Him.

If you don't have a relationship with Jesus, please talk to someone whom you trust, such as a parent or youth minister, and they will help you get started.

Keep learning and growing closer to Jesus by praying, reading your Bible, and hanging out with other Christ-followers. Jesus knows you, and He wants you to know Him and His character.

Thanks again for reading this book. May God bless you and keep you.

How to Become a Christian

You're not here by accident. God loves you. He wants you to have a personal relationship with Him through Jesus, His Son. There is just one thing that separates you from God. That one thing is sin.

The Bible describes sin in many ways. Most simply, sin is our failure to measure up to God's holiness and His righteous standards. We sin by things we do, choices we make, attitudes we show, and thoughts we entertain. We also sin when we fail to do right things. The Bible affirms our own experience— "there is no one righteous, not even one" (Romans 3:10). No matter how good we try to be, none of us does right things all the time.

People tend to divide themselves into groups—good people and bad people. But God says every person who has ever lived is a sinner, and any sin separates us from God. No matter how we might classify ourselves, this includes you and me. We are all sinners.

> For all have sinned and fall short of the glory of God.
>
> —Romans 3:23

Many people are confused about the way to God. Some think they will be punished or rewarded according to how good they are. Some think they should make things right in their lives before they try to come to God. Others find it hard to understand how Jesus could love them when other people don't seem to. But I have great news for you! God *does* love you! More than you can ever imagine! And there's nothing you can do to make Him stop! Yes, our sins demand punishment—the punishment of death and separation from God. But because of His great love, God sent His only Son Jesus to die for our sins.

> But God demonstrates his own love for us in this: While we were still sinners, Christ died for us.
>
> —Romans 5:8

For you to come to God, you have to get rid of your sin problem. But not one of us can do this in our own strength! You can't make yourself right with God by being a better person. Only God can rescue us from our sins. He is willing to do this not because of anything you can offer Him, but *just because He loves you!*

> He saved us, not because of righteous things we had done, but because of His mercy.
>
> —Titus 3:5

It's God's grace that allows you to come to Him—not your efforts to "clean up your life" or work your way to heaven. You can't earn it. It's a free gift.

> For it is by grace you have been saved, through faith—and this is not from yourselves, it is the gift of God—not by works, so that no one can boast.
>
> —Ephesians 2:8–9

For you to come to God, the penalty for your sin must be paid. God's gift to you is His Son Jesus, who paid the debt for you when He died on the Cross.

> For the wages of sin is death, but the gift of God is eternal life in Christ Jesus our Lord.
>
> —Romans 6:23

Jesus paid the price for your sin and mine by giving His life on a Cross at a place called Calvary, just outside of the city walls of Jerusalem in ancient Israel. God brought Jesus back from the dead. He provided the way for you to have a personal relationship with Him through Jesus. When we realize how deeply our sin grieves the heart of God and how desperately we need a Savior, we are ready to receive God's offer of salvation. To admit we are sinners means turning away from our sin and selfishness and turning to follow Jesus. The Bible's word for this is *repentance*—to change our thinking about how grievous sin is, so our thinking is in line with God's.

All that's left for you to do is to accept the gift that Jesus is holding out for you right now.

> If you declare with your mouth, "Jesus is Lord," and believe in your heart that God raised him from the dead, you will be saved. For it is with your heart that you believe and are justified, and it is with your mouth that you profess your faith and are saved.
>
> —Romans 10:9–10

God says that if you believe in His Son Jesus, you can live forever with Him in glory.

> For God so loved the world that He gave his one and only Son, that whoever believes in him shall not perish but have eternal life.
>
> —John 3:16

Are you ready to accept the gift of eternal life Jesus is offering you right now? Let's review what this commitment involves:

- I acknowledge I am a sinner in need of a Savior—this is to repent or turn away from sin.
- I believe in my heart that God raised Jesus from the dead—this is to trust that Jesus paid the full penalty for my sins.
- I confess Jesus as my Lord and my God—this is to surrender control of my life to Jesus.
- I receive Jesus as my Savior forever—this is to accept that God has done for me and in me what He promised.

If it is your sincere desire to receive Jesus into your heart as your personal Lord and Savior, then talk to God from your heart.

Here's a suggested prayer:

"Lord Jesus, I know I am a sinner, and I do not deserve eternal life. But I believe You died and rose from the grave to make me a new creation and to prepare me to dwell in Your presence forever. Jesus, come into my life, take control of my life, forgive my sins, and save me. I am now placing my trust in You alone for my salvation, and I accept your free gift of eternal life. Amen."

How to Share Your Faith

When engaging someone with the gospel, we use the same approach we see Jesus using in Scripture: love, listen, discern, and respond.

Love
Love comes from God
Go out of your way
Go be amongst the crowd
Change your environment

Listen
Ask questions
Listen for the heart issue
Don't defend or argue

Discern
Discernment is from the Holy Spirit
Discern the Holy Spirit's leading
What's the point of entry?

Respond
When we love, listen, and discern, we are prepared to respond, the Holy Spirit does the work, and God is glorified. Ask, "Is there anything keeping you from accepting the free gift of life in Jesus today?" You can help your friend pray to receive salvation by praying the prayer on page 76.

How to Pray for Your Friends

God is a chain breaker and, through Jesus, gives us victory over sin. Sometimes we like to hold on to our sins because they are comfortable, and we look at letting go as losing something valuable. But God has something so much better for us if we choose to surrender to His call to holiness. If one of your friends has a habit you know God wants them to let go of, ask God to help them not fear change as losing something but rather rejoice in it as gaining something better.

God, the Bible tells us that You have plans for us and those plans are for our good. My friend _____ struggles with _____(habit, addiction, temptation, attitude, etc.) On their behalf, I ask You to be the God of change in their life. Open their eyes so they no longer fear change or see it as something negative to be lost but rather can see change as something You have that is so much better for them. God, help them to give up those things that separate them from You so they can be set apart from the world for Your purposes. Amen.

Some people view holiness as having to live by boring, strict rules or, worse, being surrounded by people who act holier-than-thou as they force their standards on others. God's desire is that we balance truth and grace in love.

God, I know _____ follows after You. Help him/her know that following You does not mean living by strict rules for the sake of following rules. Show _____ how to balance grace and truth with love as they interact with our friends. Guide their words of truth so they are spoken in love. Enable them to use the art of tact so they do not make enemies but rather draw our friends into a deeper walk with You. Show me how to stand alongside them in truth while abounding in love. Amen.

As people grow more and more concerned about their personal image or move to the completely opposite and disregard what anyone thinks, there is one person we should seek to please. Our character (who we are in private or public) matters to God.

Jesus, _____ and I have placed worthless things in front of our eyes. The images, videos, games that we place before us are not honoring or pleasing to You. In fact, if I'm honest, I confess they fill our minds with lust, greed, violence, and discontentment. Show us how to encourage each other to holy living. Give us strength to make courageous choices and choose things that will please You. Amen.

**If you enjoyed this book, will you consider
sharing the message with others?**

Let us know your thoughts at info@newhopepublishers.com.
You can also let us know by visiting or sharing a photo of the
cover on our social media pages or leaving a review at
a retailer's site. All of it helps us get the message out!

Twitter.com/NewHopeBooks
Facebook.com/NewHopePublishers
Instagram.com/NewHopePublishers

— — — — — —

New Hope® Publishers is an imprint of Iron Stream Media,
which derives its name from Proverbs 27:17,
"As iron sharpens iron, so one person sharpens another."

This sharpening describes the process of discipleship,
one to another. With this in mind, Iron Stream Media
provides a variety of solutions for churches, missionaries,
and nonprofits ranging from in-depth Bible study curriculum
and Christian book publishing to custom publishing and
consultative services. Through the popular Life Bible Study
and Student Life Bible Study brands, ISM provides web-based
full-year and short-term Bible study teaching plans as well as
printed devotionals, Bibles, and discipleship curriculum.

For more information on ISM and
New Hope Publishers, please visit
IronStreamMedia.com
NewHopePublishers.com